TIMES PAST
–THE–
NORTH-EAST

*This book is part of the Times Past series, produced using photographs from the archives of the Hulton Picture Library including many from the famous **Picture Post** magazine.*

TOP: BAMBURGH SANDS, 1910. BOTTOM, LEFT TO RIGHT: PAINTING THE TEES BRIDGE, 1935; NEWCASTLE FA CUP CELEBRATIONS, 1951; PLOUGHING DEMONSTRATION, HORSLEY-ON-TYNE, 1944.

MYRIAD
LONDON

BERWICK AND ALNWICK

Berwick and its close neighbour Alnwick have both suffered from their position as border towns. Berwick changed hands between Scotland and England no fewer than 13 times. Its close neighbour Alnwick has one of the best preserved castles in Britain.

ABOVE: **BERWICK BORDER BRIDGE, 1910.** Fishermen showing their catch to a group of small boys on the beach next to the old border bridge. The oldest of Berwick's three bridges, the Berwick Border Bridge is built of red sandstone and has 15 arches. Building work on the bridge started in 1611 but progress was slow and the bridge did not open until 1624.

BELOW: **ROYAL BORDER BRIDGE, 1903.** The Flying Scotsman hurtles across the impressive 19th-century railway viaduct. Opened by Queen Victoria in 1850, the bridge was designed by Robert Stephenson.

ABOVE: **SKATING ON THE ALN**, *c*1920. A late afternoon on the frozen river Aln beneath the shadow of Alnwick castle. The imposing castle was used as a scene for Hogwarts in the film *Harry Potter and the Philosopher's Stone*.

RIGHT: **BERWICK TOWN, 1955.** One attractive feature of Berwick is the common use of pantiles for roofing – seen here in Castle Street.

LEFT: **BERWICK NEWSAGENT, 1955.** Both Scottish and English newspapers are sold throughout the border towns.

HOLY ISLAND

Holy Island or Lindisfarne is one of the most important places in the history of Christianity in Britain. In 635 Aidan established a monastery on the island. Today the ruins of a Norman priory and a castle dominate the landscape.

RIGHT: **FISHING SUCCESS, 1911.** A fisherman brings his catch ashore on the coast close to Holy Island. Lindisfarne Castle, which sits on top of the island, was originally a Tudor fort. It was converted into a home in 1903 by the architect Edwin Lutyens.

BELOW: **VISITORS TO HOLY ISLAND, 1910.** A party return across the wet sand on horse and cart after visiting the island. Holy Island is a rocky outcrop which can only be reached by a causeway at low tide.

ABOVE: **TEEING OFF, 1910.** Golfers and their caddies at the ninth tee on Bamburgh Castle golf course. The course is rated one of the most beautiful in Britain and gives glorious views across the bay to Holy Island.

RIGHT: **DAD'S ARMY, 1942.** Holy Island fishermen go through their rifle drills in front of the ruined island priory during the Second World War.

LEFT: **HOLY WATER, 1935.** Two clergymen enjoy a paddle.

Fishing and the coast

ABOVE: **WHITLEY BAY, 1925.** Whitley Bay became a popular resort for nearby Newcastle during the middle of the 19th century when a railway connected the town to the city centre. St Mary's lighthouse (just visible at the top right of the photograph) was built in 1898 on a rocky outcrop a short distance from the mainland. The lighthouse remained in operation until 1984.

RIGHT: **DARLING GRAVE, 1934.** Grace Horsley Darling (1815-1842) and her father William, keeper of the Longstone lighthouse on the Farne Islands, achieved lasting fame by their daring rescue of nine seamen whose ship had run aground on nearby rocks in 1838.

BELOW: **LIFEBOAT CREW, 1939.** The crew of the Cullercoats lifeboat *"Richard Silver Oliver"* line up for a photograph.

ABOVE: **SALMON CATCH. 1910.** Boys helping with the catch as salmon nets are hauled ashore at Tweedmouth sands. Salmon fishing with nets was once an important industry along the mouth of the Tweed but the rights to fish have gradually been bought out by rod fishermen and landowners.

ABOVE: **BRINGING IN THE CATCH, 1955.** Newbiggin by the Sea developed as a coalmining and grain exporting centre but it has always had a fishing fleet operating from small boats or "cobles". Women played a large part in the industry, baiting hooks, dragging the boats in and carrying fish.

RIGHT: **FISHWIVES, 1955.** Jane Armstrong of Newbiggin baits hooks ready for the next fishing trip. The line of baited hooks is carefully coiled so that it will not snag once thrown out of the boat.

LEFT: **FISHERMEN'S WIVES, 1926.** A group of fishermen's wives from Cullercoats wearing traditional shawls, staging an anti-strike demonstration during the General Strike.

NEWCASTLE-UPON-TYNE

Shipbuilding and engineering built Newcastle into a mighty industrial centre – and left a heritage of Georgian and Victorian architecture which graces the city to this day.

RIGHT: **VICTORIAN NEWCASTLE, 1889.** Dog Leap Stairs, near the Blackgate, is so-called because the stairs leading into this area were so narrow that a dog could leap across them.

BELOW: **WET NEWCASTLE, 1954.** The city's Georgian and Victorian buildings left a rich heritage.

BOTTOM: **TRAIN OVER TYNE, 1910.** A passenger train crosses the High Level Bridge over the Tyne, designed by Robert Stephenson and opened in 1849. The original low level bridge sited at the front of the new bridge was demolished and in its place the Armstrong swing bridge – at the time the largest swing bridge anywhere in the world – was opened in 1876.

RIGHT: **CENTRAL STATION, 1900.** Once the High Level Bridge was in place Central Station was opened in 1850 by Queen Victoria. The impressive portico was added in 1863. To the right is St Mary's church and spire.

BELOW: **GREY STREET, c1890.** Grey Street was named after British Prime Minister Earl Grey (1830-34), a Northumbrian by birth, whose 135ft (41m) monument stands at the head of the street. The elegant street – recently voted the best street in Britain in a nationwide poll – was developed in the 1830s by architects John Dobson and Richard Grainger who built much of Newcastle's central district. The handsome potico on the right is the entrance to the Theatre Royal.

BELOW RIGHT: **GREY STREET, 1939.** The grandeur of the limestone buildings and porticos of Grey Street show why the thoroughfare is so admired.

ABOVE: **THE OLD AND THE NEW, 1938.** A city shop tries to catch customers with a mix of old world charm and modern advertising.

BELOW: **SUNDAY CYCLISTS, 1938.** Cycling club members check their bikes before setting off on a Sunday bike ride around the city.

RIGHT: **HANGING UP WASHING, 1950.** Industry and housing often existed side by side in Newcastle. A woman hangs up her washing in a Tyneside street close to the entrance to a sweet factory.

Left: **TYNESIDERS, 1950.** A street scene in the West End. A long industrial history and sense of place allowed a quite distinct "Geordie" identity to develop which reflected itself both in humour and speech.

Below: **PENNY BAZAAR, 1955.** Built in the 1930s, the Grainger market is the city's oldest, located in an elegant parade in Grey Street close to the monument. It still houses a sentimental – but paying – reminder of an original Marks & Spencer penny bazaar. Michael Marks opened the first penny bazaar in Kirkgate, Leeds in 1834. His motto was "Don't ask the price – it's a penny"!

Above: **MAKING THE BEST OF IT, 1955.** After the Second World War, much of Newcastle's housing was cleared to make way for new developments. But many families remained in poor housing for years, like this family in a cottage in Back Hammond Street which had been condemned in 1938.

THE TYNE

*For centuries the river has played a key role in
Newcastle's history. Docks were built along the
quayside to carry away coal from the region's mines
and later a huge shipbuilding industry with yards such
as Swan Hunter at Wallsend developed.*

ABOVE: **TYNE BRIDGE, 1954.** A Sunday afternoon stroll along the
quayside – the oldest part of Newcastle and, until the 19th
century, its main commercial centre. In the background is the
familiar arch of the Tyne Bridge and behind that the Swing
Bridge and the High Level Bridge.

RIGHT: **TYNE BRIDGE, 1928.** The Tyne Bridge seen shortly before
its opening in 1928. When built, this was the largest single
span bridge in the world and it was used as a prototype for
the much larger Sydney Harbour Bridge.

ABOVE: **DOCKSIDE AREA, 1938.** A terraced street south of the river with the derricks of a shipbuilding yard looming at the end of the street, seemingly almost within touching distance.

BELOW LEFT: **QUAYSIDE, 1954.** The traditional Sunday market held on the Quayside is something of a north-east institution. The first record of a quayside market appears in 1736 – and the market continues to this day, attracting up to 100,000 people every week.

ABOVE: **TYNE STREET, 1950.** Looking towards the Tyne at Scotswood. In the early part of the 20th century, Scotswood was a by-word for heavy industry. The giant Armstrong and Whitworth (later Vickers) factory stretched along the western riverfront for more than a mile and a half.

JARROW

Thanks to its famous hunger march, Jarrow became a symbol of the industrial decay of the 1930s. It is a town with a long history – from the Anglo-Saxon monk the Venerable Bede, through to shipbuilding, steelmaking and the Jarrow Crusades of the 1930s.

ABOVE: **BREAKER'S YARD, 1924.** HMS Lion docked at Jarrow ready for the breaker's yard. The Lion was badly damaged in the Battle of Jutland in 1916.

BELOW: **TYNESIDE GREASER, 1954.** Working on engine turbines at a shipbuilders' yard.

ABOVE: **JARROW SHIPYARD, 1939.** The liner "Berengaria", pride of the Cunard Line, is taken to the breaker's yard in Jarrow to be dismantled. Due to the outbreak of war, it wasn't until 1946 that the remains of the hull were finally broken up.

LEFT: **JARROW STEELWORKERS, 1939.** The Palmer Steelworks and Shipyard closed in the 1930s with the result that 74 per cent of all the workers in Jarrow were unemployed. In reaction, the workers organised the Jarrow Crusade – a march to London to draw attention to their plight. Although other steelworks were opened in the town, they had all eventually closed by the 1990s.

ABOVE: **JARROW FOOD STOP, 1936.** Marchers stop for a sandwich on their month-long walk to London to present a petition to Parliament drawing attention to growing unemployment in the north-east. Two hundred men marched 300 miles from Jarrow, led by their local MP Ellen Wilkinson.

RIGHT: **JARROW STREET, 1947.** By the time this photograph of a busy shopping street in central Jarrow was taken the town had a population of over 30,000 people.

FROM WALLSEND TO THE SEA

The towns of the lower Tyne and its estuary – Wallsend, North and South Shields and Tynemouth – developed their own distinct identity, even though many gradually merged with the larger Newcastle conurbation.

ABOVE: **TYNEMOUTH BEACH, 1890.** Busy Long Sands beach in the late Victorian period. The dominant Plaza building towers over the beach. The Plaza opened in 1878 as a winter garden and aquarium complete with its own swimming pool which converted into a skating rink in winter. Fire badly damaged the already decaying building in 1996 and it had to be demolished. In the distance is St George's parish church. Missing from the foreground of this picture is the rock pool which was built as a swimming pool in 1925 and converted back to a rock pool in 1996.

LEFT: **SOUTH SHIELDS, 1890.** King Street, the town's main shopping thoroughfare looking down towards the railway bridge with a horse-drawn tram in the foreground. Crofton's drapery store stands on the left-hand corner.

RIGHT: **AFTER WORK, 1939.** A mass of workers leaving the Wallsend shipyard at the end of the working day. These were some of the lucky workers still employed in shipbuilding. At this time, 21 per cent of the Tyneside workforce were unemployed – compared with 13 per cent in the rest of the country.

ABOVE: **DOWN THE TYNE, 1950.** Two fishing boats steam out to sea passing the rugged Tynemouth priory on the headland overlooking the estuary.

BELOW: **WALLSEND, 1950.** A bustling scene shows that the Tyne was still extremely busy, even in the 1950s.

SUNDERLAND

Sunderland has a proud tradition of coalmining and shipbuilding – and a longstanding rivalry with its neighbouring conurbation on the Tyne.

RIGHT: **WINTER GARDENS,** *c*1930s. The Winter Garden in Mowbray Park became one of Sunderland's most popular buildings in the 1930s. A parachute mine in 1941 severely damaged the building and it had to be demolished. A museum and library were built on the site in 1960 and in 2002 a new £20m development with a spectacular new winter garden as its centrepiece was opened in the park.

LEFT: **FAWCETT STREET, 1910.** In the 19th century Fawcett Street was a smart residential area but by the early years of the 20th century it had become the centre of Sunderland's commercial and business area. Electric-powered trams like those shown were introduced in 1900.

ABOVE: **HIGH STREET WEST,** *c*1905. One of the busiest streets in town in the early 20th century, containing shops such as Joplings, Sunderland's longest-established store, which moved here from High Street East in 1919. The store later relocated to its present site in John Street in 1956.

LEFT: **OLD SUNDERLAND, 1889.**
A group of women and
children sitting around on
the steps of a shop in an old
area of the town.

BELOW: **GOODBYE SUNDERLAND,
1948.** In 1948 a new trade
agreement was set up to
supply Denmark with coal
from the north-east. It was
agreed to send Harry
Wilkins, a local coalminer,
with the first ship as an
ambassador for the town.
Here, Harry waves a last
farewell as the *"Kentucky"*
makes its way under the
Wear Bridge.

BOTTOM: **ROKER BEACH AND
PIER, 1936.** The lighthouse
and pier were opened in 1903.
During the 1920s the
promenade was extended to
Seaburn. Illuminations
started on the seafront in
1937 and became an annual
event until 1959. They were
revived again in the 1980s.

BELOW LEFT: **LEAVING PORT, 1948.**
A cargo boat leaves
Wearmouth Staithes in
atmospheric mist.

Coal Mining

One hundred years ago it would have been hard to imagine the north-east without a coal industry – now there are no mines left. But memories of mining and its way of life still run deep.

BELOW: LEAD KINDLY LIGHT, 1939. Miner Tommy Shotton collects his miner's lamp before beginning the night shift.

BOTTOM: HARD GRAFT, 1951. Miners hard at work in cramped conditions at the pit face at Ellington Colliery, Northumberland.

LEFT: **SLAG HEAP SEARCH, 1938.** Times were often desperate when miners were on strike or "short-time". These men are combing the slag or waste heaps from the mine for individual lumps of coal.

RIGHT: **THE KIST, 1934.** In a Durham mine, a deputy makes out his report at the "kist" or station after inspecting the coalface to see all is safe before a shift starts.

RIGHT BELOW: **PIT PONY, 1951.** Miners make a fuss of one of the 85 pit ponies kept in underground stables at Ellington Colliery, Northumberland. The ponies were used to haul coal, stones and supplies.

ABOVE: **PAY SLIPS, 1950.** Miners who have just completed a shift at Heworth Colliery near Newcastle compare wage slips.

LEFT: **WASHING FOR DINNER, 1935.** A miner from Ashington Colliery washing in a tin bath in front of the fire.

DURHAM

The dramatic city of Durham is dominated by its ancient castle and cathedral. In the recent past, coal, steel and rail have contributed to the fortunes of the town.

ABOVE: **DURHAM, 1910.** A panoramic view of the city, with a steam train crossing the railway viaduct. Situated on a magnificent rocky outcrop above the River Wear, the castle and cathedral loom over the town.

BELOW: **DURHAM CASTLE, *c*1930.** Visitors view the castle from Framwellgate Bridge. Many of the old buildings in the Framwellgate area were demolished in the 1930s because of their poor condition. In 1986 the cathedral and castle were designated a World Heritage Site.

LEFT AND BELOW: In 1939 *Picture Post* magazine sent journalists to Durham to report on unemployment and in 1944 to cover wage cuts in the Durham coalfield. The photographs show the almost deserted streets of the city during the war and children in the street. Mining had been in decline throughout the 1930s and although the status of coalminers was boosted during the war the fragile economy led to wage cuts. In 1947 the industry was eventually taken into public ownership – a move which had been advocated as early as 1919.

Rural life

RIGHT: **VILLAGE GREEN, 1950.** A woman fills a bucket with water at a tap on the village green at Wark. Wark was originally the capital of North Tynedale and its castle was vital to control this lawless border region. All that remains of the castle today is a large rock and rubble mound overlooking the Tweed.

BELOW: **DANCING WOMEN, 1953.** Country dancing by members of the Eastgate Women's Institute in Weardale. The local Institute had 31 members. Tea hostesses at monthly meetings have to bring water in buckets from the village pump.

BOTTOM: **STOOKING BARLEY, 1939.** At Howick Seahouses farm, the owner and two of his workers arrange barley into "stooks" to dry.

ABOVE: **WEARHEAD, 1941.** Wearhead stands on the north bank of the Wear at the confluence of the Kilhope and Burnhope Water. Famous as the birthplace of the railway – the first trip from Etherley Colliery on the Stockton to Darlington railway took place on September 27 1825 – it was also a centre of lead-mining in the 19th century.

LEFT: **BELFORD VILLAGE, 1941.** A cottage in Clark Place with Belford church in the background.

BELOW: **BAGPIPES, 1950.** An elderly man shows grandchildren his Northumbrian pipes. The Northumbrian pipes – or smallpipes – issue a lilting, evocative sound and have been in use in the north-east since at least the 17th century. Unlike many other types of bagpipe they are not inflated by mouth but by using a small bellows mounted under the player's arm.

MIDDLESBROUGH

At the beginning of the 19th century, Middlesbrough was a farming area on the banks of the Tees. Then the Stockton to Darlington railway was extended and Middlesbrough grew into a massive coal port – made even larger by the discovery of iron ore nearby.

ABOVE: **MIDDLESBROUGH, 1945.** Post-war reconstruction got under way in the town with a massive survey into its future development. Here, young women head off to the Town Plan exhibition. In one week, more than 10,000 people viewed maps and models of the Middlesbrough of the future. Townsfolk were quizzed on their attitudes, needs and desires with regard to the location of new factories, housing and schools. Pollution was high on the agenda: at this time, 450 tons of soot per square mile fell on homes in Middlesbrough each year.

ABOVE AND RIGHT: **STREET SCENES, 1945.** Children in Middlesbrough play in streets dominated by the town's industry. Such was its rapid growth, Middlesbrough was described as "the town that grew one thousand times in one hundred years". Until the end of the war it retained the grid pattern set up by its founder, Joseph Pease.

ABOVE AND LEFT: **STEELWORKS 1948 AND 1961.** After the discovery of local iron ore in 1850 a blast furnace was set up in 1851. Middlesbrough moved rapidly from coal mining to being an iron, then steel, town. In 1875, the first steel plant was set up by local ironmaster John Vaughan. Soon the Tees became known as "steel river".

ABOVE: **SINKING FOUNDATIONS, 1933.** Tons of clay are blown out as foundations are sunk for the Newport Bridge. Designed by engineers Mott, Nay and Anderson, the Newport Bridge over the Tees was the country's first lift bridge when it was opened in 1934. The central section was raised and lowered to allow ships to pass underneath. The nearby Transporter Bridge was built in 1911.

TEESSIDE AND BEYOND

Right: **REDCAR PROMENADE, 1890.** In the late 19th century Redcar developed rapidly as a seaside resort – thanks to its position on the coast a few miles south of the mouth of the Tees. Its prosperity was also helped by the popularity of its racecourse. All that remains of the elegant pier today is a rump of concrete.

Below: **WOOL FACTORY, 1958.** Workers making up shade cards at Patons and Baldwins wool factory in West Hartlepool.

Above: **MARKET DAY, 1950.** Stockton-on-Tees market has operated here since the Middle Ages helping Stockton to retain much of its essential market town character. The distinctive Dutch-style town hall with clock and spire is over 250 years old.

Left: **REPLICA ROCKET, 1935.** Workers at Robert Stephenson and Co of Darlington constructing a full-size replica of Stephenson's famous train the *Rocket* for the Science Museum in London. Robert's father, George Stephenson, had pioneered the use of steam engines on the world's first railway – the Stockton to Darlington.

Below: **LNER SNOWPLOUGH, 1936.** No problem with "wrong type of snow on the line" with this monster 12ft (3.6m)-high snowplough seen here at Darlington and weighing in at 20 tons. Two engines and two ploughs are mounted back-to-back so that the vehicle can operate more easily in both directions.

Below: **SCHOOLBOY FIREMEN, 1933.** A group of local schoolboys get some practical, hands-on experience shovelling coal from the tender at the LNER Museum in York. The train they are driving is an LNER Shire engine.

Football

*North-east football means far more than the support for one team —
it also involves fierce rivalry between the various towns and cities
of the region and pride in their local heroes.*

RIGHT: WOR JACKIE, 1952. Newcastle United legend Jackie Milburn (1924-1988) watches the ball go over the bar in the 1952 FA Cup Final against Arsenal. Milburn helped the Magpies to a 1-0 victory. Milburn made a total of 494 appearances for Newcastle scoring 239 goals.

BELOW: BACK TO HEALTH, 1958. Manchester United footballer Bobby Charlton gets back into gentle training with some young fans in his home town of Ashington following his recovery from the Munich air crash.

RIGHT: FRIENDLY GAME, 1950. Henshaw, captain of the Nigerian national team, leads his players out on to the field in a match against Bishop Auckland. Although this was a "friendly" match – and one of the first times any African football team had toured Britain – Bishop Auckland would have been tough opponents for the Nigerian team since at this time they made regular appearances in amateur cup finals. As can be seen, some Nigerians played without boots, using ankle straps instead.

ABOVE: ST JAMES' PARK, NEWCASTLE, 1930. Newcastle FC was formed when Newcastle West End and Newcastle East End merged in 1892 and the more successful East End moved into the West End's ground at St James' Park. In 1905 the ground was substantially redeveloped to hold 60,000 fans. It remained largely unaltered for the next 70 years.

LEFT: NEWCASTLE CUP WIN, 1951. Captain Joe Harvey, holding the cup, celebrates with his Newcastle team mates their win over Blackpool in the FA Cup Final – the first half of their FA Cup "double". Jackie Milburn, who scored both goals, is being congratulated by Ernie Taylor.

BELOW: MANNION AND THE LADS, 1951. A group of young boys test out their football skills on the Middlesbrough streets with their local team idol, Wilf Mannion (1918-2000). He played 368 times for Middlesbrough, scoring 110 goals..

ABOVE: SUNDERLAND FC, 1926. From the back row and from left to right are: McGorian, England, McInroy, Henderson, Creswell (captain), Andrews, Kelly, Marshall, Gurney, Coglin and Ellis. Sunderland are winners of six league championships and two FA Cups.

Above: **ALL ROADS LEAD TO WASHINGTON, 1960.** Village blacksmith Jim Dobson busy at work shoeing a carthorse in Washington. The ancestors of George Washington, the first president of the USA, hailed from the town.

Published in 2011 by Myriad Books Limited
35 Bishopsthorpe Road, London SE26 4PA

Photographs copyright Getty Images
Text © copyright Myriad Books Limited

ISBN 1 84746 260 x
EAN 978 1 84746 260 2

Designed by Jerry Goldie

Printed in China